SPORTS SUPERSTARS

THIS EDITION
Produced for DK by WonderLab Group LLC
Jennifer Emmett, Erica Green, Kate Hale, *Founders*

Editor Maya Myers; **Photography Editor** Kelley Miller; **Managing Editor** Rachel Houghton;
Designers Project Design Company; **Researcher** Michelle Harris; **Copy Editor** Lori Merritt;
Indexer Connie Binder; **Proofreader** Susan K. Hom; **Series Reading Specialist** Dr. Jennifer Albro

First American Edition, 2025
Published in the United States by DK Publishing, a division of Penguin Random House LLC
1745 Broadway, 20th Floor, New York, NY 10019

Copyright © 2025 Dorling Kindersley Limited
25 26 27 10 9 8 7 6 5 4 3 2 1
001-345864-August/2025

All rights reserved.
Without limiting the rights under the copyright reserved above, no part of this publication may be reproduced, stored in or introduced
into a retrieval system, or transmitted, in any form, or by any means (electronic, mechanical, photocopying, recording, or otherwise),
without the prior written permission of the copyright owner.

DK values and supports copyright. Thank you for respecting intellectual property laws by not reproducing, scanning or distributing
any part of this publication by any means without permission. By purchasing an authorised edition, you are supporting writers and
artists and enabling DK to continue to publish books that inform and inspire readers. No part of this publication may be used
or reproduced in any manner for the purpose of training artificial intelligence technologies or systems. In accordance with
Article 4(3) of the DSM Directive 2019/790, DK expressly reserves this work from the text and data mining exception.

Published in Great Britain by Dorling Kindersley Limited

A catalog record for this book is available from the Library of Congress.
HC ISBN: 978-0-5939-6621-1
PB ISBN: 978-0-5939-6620-4

DK books are available at special discounts when purchased in bulk for sales promotions, premiums, fund-raising, or educational use.
For details, contact:
DK Publishing Special Markets, 1745 Broadway, 20th Floor, New York, NY 10019
SpecialSales@dk.com

Printed and bound in China
Super Readers Lexile® levels 620L to 790L
Lexile® is the registered trademark of MetaMetrics, Inc. Copyright © 2024 MetaMetrics, Inc. All rights reserved.

The publisher would like to thank the following for their kind permission to reproduce their images:
a=above; c=center; b=below; l=left; r=right; t=top; b/g=background
Alamy Stock Photo: Associated Press / Aijaz Rahi 32b, Associated Press / Jonathan Hayward 41b, DPA / Sven Hoppe 44-45,
Juergen Hasenkopf 42-43, 43b, PA Images / John Walton 43t; **Dreamstime.com:** Photolight 10-11, Leigh Warner 18-19, Lawrence
Weslowski Jr 28-29, 30-31; **Getty Images:** AFP / Angela Weiss 15t, AFP / Money Sharma 32-33, 33b, AFP / Paul Crock 42b, AFP / Paul
Ellis 33t, Manuel Queimadelos Alonso 12, Anadolu 26b, Naomi Baker 24t, Al Bello 15b, Bettmann 17t, 31c, Shaun Botterill 7t, 37b, Dylan
Buell 45t, 45b, Andy Cheung 7b, Corbis Sport / Tim Clayton 38b, 38-39, Kevin C. Cox 4-5, DeFodi Images 6, 8cr, 9t, Julian Finney 8t,
Gamma-Keystone / Keystone-France 25cr, Jeff Gross 13t, Matthias Hangst 26-27, Harry How 34c, Hulton Archive / David Rogers 19t,
Hulton Archive / Derek Hudson 20-21, Hulton Archive / Photo File 30t, Hulton Archive / Todd Warshaw 40, ISI Photos / John Todd 13b,
Ryan Kang 16, Kyodo News 22, 41t, Christopher Lee 19b, Bryn Lennon 25cla, Ian MacNicol 23b, David Madison 11t, Major League
Baseball Platinum / National Baseball Hall of Fame Library 31t, Mondadori Portfolio 3, Dean Mouhtaropoulos 24b, National Basketball
Association / Cooper Neill 36b, NurPhoto 24-25, Michael Owens 28b, Alex Pantling 7cra, Tom Pennington 21t, Doug Pensinger 45m,
Mickey Pfleger 17b, Popperfoto / Paul Popper 1, 11b, Popperfoto / Rolls Press 10t, Adam Pretty 20b, Ezra Shaw 20c, Alex Slitz 26t,
29b, Sports Illustrated / Andy Hayt 36t, Sports Illustrated / Kohjiro Kinno 14, Sports Illustrated Classic / David Sherman 37t,
Sports Illustrated Classic / Eric Schweikardt 10b, Michael Steele 21c, 23t, Ric Tapia 9b, Universal Images Group / Universal History
Archive 30b, Louis Van Oeyen / WRHS 29t; **Getty Images / iStock:** E+ / Dmytro Aksonov 16-17, 36-37;
Shutterstock.com: BPI 18, Cinema Legacy Collection / THA 44b

Cover images: *Front:* **Dreamstime.com:** Mark J. Grenier t, Sergei Kuzmin (Texture);
Getty Images: AFP / Franck Fife bl, AFP / Jonathan Nackstrand cr, Laurence Griffiths c, Ronald Martinez cl,
MB Media / Pablo Morano br; *Back:* **Dreamstime.com:** Taras Adamovych cla, Veronika Oliinyk cl, Tartilastock cra

www.dk.com

This book was made with Forest
Stewardship Council™ certified
paper – one small step in DK's
commitment to a sustainable future.
Learn more at www.dk.com/uk/
information/sustainability

SPORTS SUPERSTARS

Eric Zweig

Contents

6	Game On!
8	Super Soccer
14	Fantastic Football
18	Remarkable Rugby
20	Summertime Stars
26	Paralympic Power
28	Big-Time Baseball
32	Cracking Cricket
34	Basketball's Best
38	Winter Wonders
42	Terrific Tennis
44	Solo Standouts
46	Glossary
47	Index
48	Quiz

Alexi Salamone

Game On!

Bzzzz! The players are ready. The crowd is on its feet. The action is about to start…

All around the world, people love sports. Thousands of people fill stadiums. They tune in on TV to watch their favorite athletes in action. Few things bring people together like cheering for the home team.

Spanish fans at the 2024 Olympic Games

The Italian team celebrating their 2006 FIFA World Cup win

Panipak Wongpattanakit of Thailand

People also love to talk about sports. Who's the greatest athlete now? Who's the GOAT—the greatest of all time?

Watching sports superstars can inspire us. Reading about them can, too. Let's go!

Rebecca Andrade of Brazil

Lionel Messi in the final match of the FIFA World Cup 2022

Super Soccer

Soccer, or football, is the world's most popular sport. It's played all over the globe and by hundreds of millions of people! The biggest international event in soccer is the World Cup. The Brazilian men's team has won the World Cup a record five times. The American women's team has won the World Cup four times. They have also won five Olympic gold medals.

Lionel Messi

Many people consider Lionel Messi the greatest soccer player of recent times. He's quick with his feet and precise with his passes. Messi is from Argentina. But he played most of his career in Spain. He won the World Cup with Argentina in 2022.

Bend It Like Beckham

British soccer star David Beckham had a special skill. He could curl his free kicks around a wall of defenders. "Bend It Like Beckham" became a popular phrase. It's also the title of a movie about girls playing soccer.

Pelé

His real name was Edson Arantes do Nascimento. People knew him as Pelé. It means "the one who is extraordinary." Some consider him soccer's GOAT. He was known for scoring spectacular goals. Pelé grew up in Brazil. He learned to play soccer using a grapefruit for a ball. Pelé began his professional career at age 15. He played for 21 years. Pelé played 1,367 professional games. He scored a record 1,283 goals. He's the only player to have played on three winning World Cup teams.

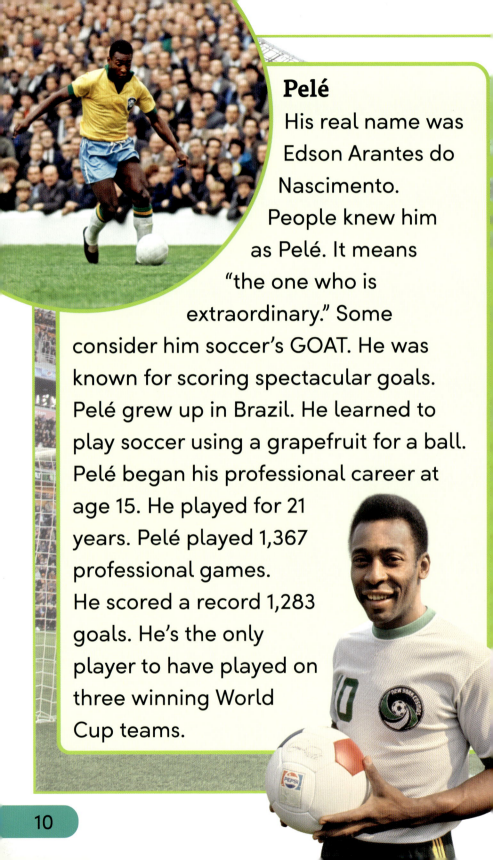

Mia Hamm

At 19, Mia Hamm was the youngest player on the US team at the first Women's World Cup in 1991. Hamm went on to win two World Cup titles and two Olympic gold medals with the US team.

Bobby Moore

Bobby Moore was known for his ability to quickly see and understand patterns in the play. In 1966, he was team captain when England won the World Cup. Pelé called Moore the greatest defender he ever played against.

Cristiano Ronaldo

Portugal's Cristiano Ronaldo has starred for his national team since he was 18. He's been team captain since 2008. Ronaldo has played for club teams in Portugal, England, Spain, Italy, and Saudi Arabia. Ronaldo is a hard worker with great speed. He's played over 1,200 career games. He's scored more than 900 career goals. His teams have won many league and European championships.

Marta

Marta Vieira da Silva of Brazil is known simply as Marta. She was the first player to score at five different World Cup tournaments. That feat was later matched by Christine Sinclair of Canada and by Cristiano Ronaldo at the men's World Cup. Marta was named FIFA Player of the Year six times.

Record Crowd

At the final game of the 1999 Women's World Cup, more than 90,000 fans packed the Rose Bowl stadium. This was a worldwide attendance record for women's sports. The US beat China 5-4. All the points were scored on penalty kicks.

Fantastic Football

Football is America's game. (Canadians love football, too.) The National Football League (NFL) has 32 teams. At the end of the season, the champions are crowned in the Super Bowl. More than 100 million people watch the Super Bowl on TV each year.

A quarterback leads a team's offense. The quarterback needs to know what everybody else is doing on the field. A football team also needs running backs to carry the ball. They need receivers to catch it.

Brady's Big Numbers
Tom Brady started 333 regular-season games in his career. His teams won 251 of them. He also completed 7,753 passes for 89,214 yards. All those numbers are NFL records.

Tom Brady

Tom Brady is the most successful quarterback in football history. He was great at spotting an open player and throwing the football quickly. Brady played in the NFL from 2001 through 2023. In 20 seasons with the New England Patriots, he led them to nine Super Bowls and won six. Brady won a seventh Super Bowl with the Tampa Bay Buccaneers. No other player has won more than five Super Bowls.

Patrick Mahomes

Patrick Mahomes is the best player in the NFL today. He's the quarterback of the Kansas City Chiefs. Mahomes is fast. His speed helps him get away from the defense. He also has a strong arm for throwing the football. Between 2018 and 2025, he led the Chiefs to five Super Bowls. They won three.

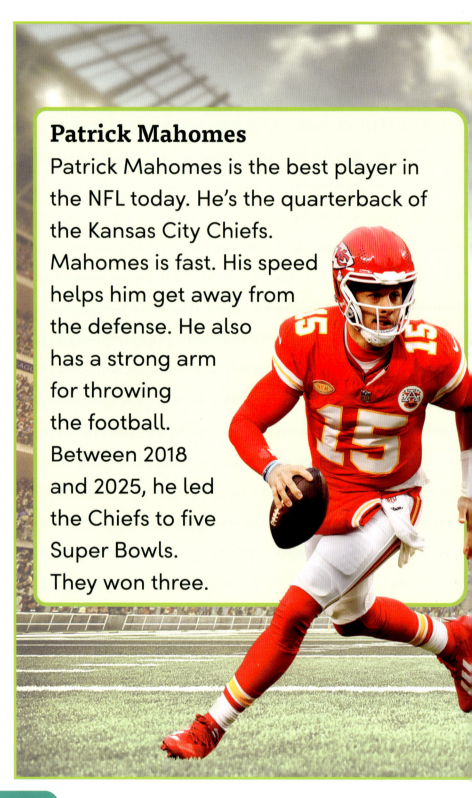

Jim Brown

Jim Brown might be football's GOAT. He played nine seasons with the Cleveland Browns, from 1957 to 1965. He led all running backs in rushing yards eight times! Brown is the only player in NFL history to average more than 100 yards rushing per game for his career.

Jerry Rice

Jerry Rice played 20 seasons in the NFL, from 1985 to 2004. He caught a record 1,549 passes. His 22,895 receiving yards are 5,000 yards more than any other player.

Remarkable Rugby

Rugby is an extremely physical game. Players carry the ball and kick it. When the ball is being carried, it can't be thrown forward to a player in front of the ball carrier.

Jonah Lomu

New Zealand's Jonah Lomu is one of rugby's GOATs. He set the all-time Rugby World Cup scoring record of 15 tries. He had seven in 1995 and eight in 1999. Bryan Habana of South Africa tied Lomu's record at his third World Cup in 2015.

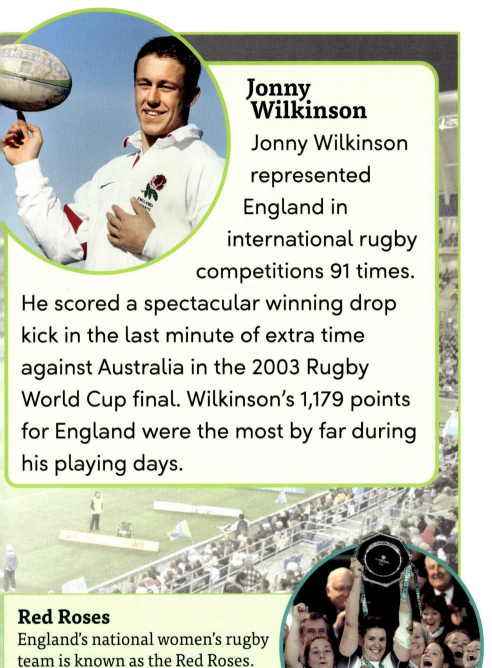

Jonny Wilkinson

Jonny Wilkinson represented England in international rugby competitions 91 times. He scored a spectacular winning drop kick in the last minute of extra time against Australia in the 2003 Rugby World Cup final. Wilkinson's 1,179 points for England were the most by far during his playing days.

Red Roses

England's national women's rugby team is known as the Red Roses. As of 2024, they've won the Women's Six Nations championship 20 times out of 29 tournaments.

Summertime Stars

The Summer Olympics is one of the biggest sporting events in the world. The first Modern Olympic Games were held in Athens in 1896. They were patterned on sports events held in ancient Greece. Traditionally, the Summer Olympics are held every four years. Gold, silver, and bronze medals are awarded to the top three finishers in every Olympic event.

Michael Phelps

Over four Olympics, from 2004 through 2016, American swimmer Michael Phelps won the most medals in Olympic history. He won 23 gold medals, three silver, and two bronze.

Katie Ledecky

No female swimmer has won more medals than Katie Ledecky of the US. At four Olympics, from 2012 through 2024, she has earned nine gold medals, four silver, and one bronze.

Sarah Storey

The UK's Sarah Storey competed at her ninth Paralympic Games in Paris in 2024. She began competing as a swimmer. Later, she switched to cycling. Storey has won 30 medals, including 19 gold medals.

Track and field includes running, jumping, throwing, and walking events. Together, they're known as athletics.

Usain Bolt

Jamaica's Usain Bolt moved like lightning! He won Olympic gold medals in the 100-meter and 200-meter races in 2008, 2012, and 2016. He also won gold twice in the 4x100-meter relay. Bolt holds the world record time of 9.58 seconds in the 100 meters.

Nafissatou Thiam

Nafissatou Thiam of Belgium is the first athlete to win three Olympic gold medals in a multisport event. Her speciality is the heptathlon. It's made up of seven different events. Thiam won her record-setting third medal in Paris in 2024.

Mo Farah

Mo Farah is a long-distance runner. He was born in Somalia but competed for the UK. He won Olympic gold medals in the 5,000-meter and 10,000-meter races in 2012 and 2016. Farah and Finland's Lasse Virén (1972 and 1976) are the only runners to have won this pair of races twice.

Simone Biles

American Simone Biles is the world's best artistic gymnast. She won four gold medals at the 2016 Olympics. In 2021, she struggled with "the twisties." It made her lose awareness of her body in the air. But in 2024, Biles won another three golds, for a total of 11 Olympic medals. She also has 30 medals from World Championships. There are five gymnastic moves named after Biles, including some that only she can do.

A Cycling Pair

British cyclist Jason Kenny competed at four Olympics. His seven gold medals are a British record. So are his nine total medals. Jason is married to cyclist Laura Kenny. She won five golds and one silver in her Olympic career.

Abebe Bikila

Abebe Bikila of Ethiopia was the first man to win the Olympic marathon twice. He won the race in 1960 running barefoot through the streets of Rome. He won again in Tokyo in 1964 wearing running shoes.

Archer Sheetal Devi of India

Paralympic Power

Athletes with disabilities have been competing in sports for more than 100 years. The first competition for wheelchair athletes was held in England in 1948. The Paralympic Games began in Rome in 1960. As of 2024, there are 22 Paralympic summer sports and six winter sports.

Goalball
Goalball is a sport for athletes who are visually impaired. It's been part of the Paralympics since 1976. Teams are made up of six players. Three members play at a time. The object is to roll a ball into the opposing team's net to score points.

Jonnie Peacock

British sprinter Jonnie Peacock raced at his fourth Paralympic Games in Paris in 2024. He won gold medals in the 100-meter race in 2012 and 2016. Peacock runs with a prosthesis known as a blade for the bottom of his right leg.

Big-Time Baseball

Baseball is known as America's National Pastime. It's popular in other countries, too. Major League Baseball started in the 1870s, but new stars keep fans on the edge of their seats!

Shohei Ohtani

Shohei Ohtani is the most famous player in baseball today. He's from Japan. He's been playing in the US since 2018. Ohtani is one of the game's top sluggers and one of the best pitchers. He can throw a ball more than 100 miles per hour (160 km/h). He hits home runs nearly 500 feet (152 m). He was the first player in baseball history to hit more than 50 home runs and steal more than 50 bases in the same season.

Babe Ruth

Babe Ruth started as a pitcher in 1914. He was also a great hitter. Ruth had super-fast reflexes. He set hitting records that seemed unbreakable! Ruth's 60 home runs for the New York Yankees in 1927 were a Major League record for 34 years. He hit 714 home runs in his career. Only two players have ever hit more. Hank Aaron hit 755 homers, and Barry Bonds hit 762.

Other Great Stars

Today's best baseball players include:
Aaron Judge, New York Yankees
Mookie Betts, Los Angeles Dodgers
Ronald Acuña Jr., Atlanta Braves
Gunnar Henderson, Baltimore Orioles
Bobby Witt Jr., Kansas City Royals.

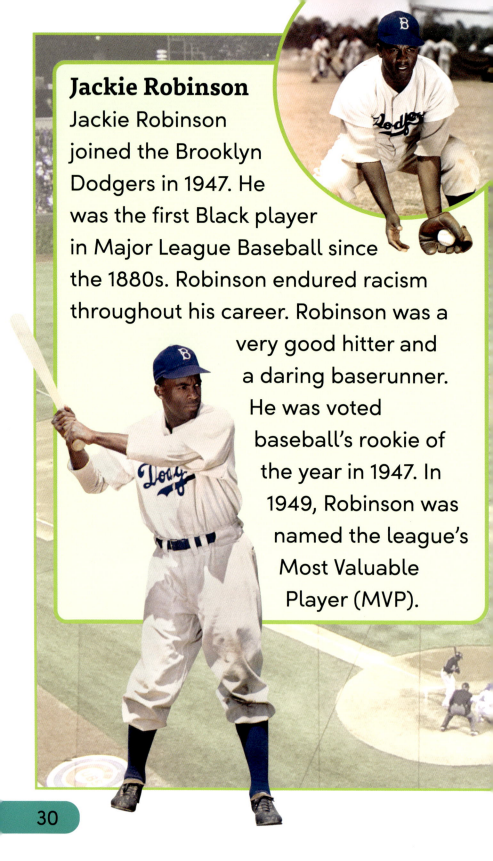

Jackie Robinson

Jackie Robinson joined the Brooklyn Dodgers in 1947. He was the first Black player in Major League Baseball since the 1880s. Robinson endured racism throughout his career. Robinson was a very good hitter and a daring baserunner. He was voted baseball's rookie of the year in 1947. In 1949, Robinson was named the league's Most Valuable Player (MVP).

Josh Gibson

Batter Up!
In 2024, Major League Baseball added statistics from the Negro Leagues to its record book. Ty Cobb, who played from 1905 to 1928, used to be the career leader in batting average. His lifetime average was .367. Now, the leader is Josh Gibson. Gibson hit .372 from 1930 to 1946.

Willie Mays
Willie Mays hit 660 career home runs. He was also great playing defense in center field. Mays played baseball with style and joy. He greeted people with a friendly, "Say Hey!" People called him "the Say Hey Kid"! Many think he's baseball's GOAT.

Cracking Cricket

Cricket is the world's second-most popular sport. Worldwide, there are said to be 3.5 billion soccer fans and 2.5 billion cricket fans. Cricket is most popular in the UK, Australia, India, Pakistan, South Africa, and the West Indies.

Sachin Tendulkar

India's Sachin Tendulkar is one of cricket's GOATs. Active from 1988 to 2013, he's a modern legend of the game. Many consider him the greatest batsman of all time. As of 2024, Tendulkar's 100 international centuries (100 runs in a single game) are 20 more than anyone else in history.

Joe Root

A lot was expected from Joe Root at a very young age. He continues to live up to the hype! Root made his international Test debut in 2012. He captained England's Test team from 2017 to 2022. He holds England's record for most runs in the history of Test cricket. Root's 35 centuries in Test cricket through 2024 rank sixth in history. He's considered one of the greatest batsmen of his era.

World Cup Cricket

There have been 13 World Cup tournaments for men since 1975. There have been 12 for women since 1973. Australia's women's team has won the World Cup seven times. Australia's men's team has won it six times.

Basketball's Best

Basketball was invented in the US in the late 19th century. The game was soon popular all around the world. The National Basketball Association (NBA) was founded in 1946. It took its current name in 1949. Since 1997, women have played in the WNBA.

LeBron James
LeBron James is the NBA's all-time scoring leader. He was only 18 when he began his pro career in 2003. LeBron combines power with speed. He's the only player in NBA history to score over 40,000 points. He's also great at passing the ball.

Sheryl Swoopes

Sheryl Swoopes was the first player signed by the WNBA. Swoopes played from 1997 to 2008, and again in 2011. Swoopes was a three-time league MVP. She was also the first female player to have a shoe named after her: "Air Swoopes."

Michael Jordan

Who is basketball's GOAT? Many fans, players, and experts think it's Michael Jordan. Jordan ranks fifth in points in NBA history. He was also an excellent defensive player. He could jump like an acrobat. That's why his line of shoes is called "Air Jordan." Jordan played 13 seasons with the Chicago Bulls between 1984 and 1998. He won five MVP awards. Jordan led the Bulls to six NBA championships and was named Finals MVP all six times.

Worldwide

NBA teams play mainly in the US. But some of the best NBA players come from all around the world. Nikola Jokić comes from Serbia. Giannis Antetokounmpo is from Greece. Victor Wembanyama comes from France. Shai Gilgeous-Alexander is from Canada.

Shai Gilgeous-Alexander

Caitlin Clark

Caitlin Clark is the highest scorer—man or woman—in college basketball history. In four years at the University of Iowa, Clark scored 3,951 points. In 2024, she was voted Rookie of the Year for the WNBA.

Patrick Anderson

Canadian Patrick Anderson lost both his legs below the knee in an accident when he was nine. He began playing wheelchair basketball a year later. Anderson led Canada to Paralympic gold medals in 2000, 2004, and 2012. He played with the Canadian team in Paris in 2024.

Winter Wonders

The first Winter Olympics were held in 1924. Norway has won more Winter Olympic medals of every color than any other country. Through 2022, that includes 148 golds, 133 silvers, and 124 bronze.

Shaun White

As a young boy, Shaun White survived two heart operations. He took up snowboarding when he was six years old. He was only 13 when he became a professional snowboarder. He was an amazing jumper. With his head of thick, red hair, he became known as "the Flying Tomato." He won gold medals at the Winter Olympics in 2006, 2010, and 2018.

Marit Bjørgen

Norway's Marit Bjørgen has won more medals than any athlete at the Winter Olympics. The cross-country skier won eight golds, four silvers, and three bronze. She competed at every winter Olympics from 2002 through 2018.

Wayne Gretzky

From 1979 until 1999, Wayne Gretzky was the National Hockey League's hottest thing on ice. Gretzky won the scoring trophy a record 10 times. He won the NHL's MVP award a record nine times. Gretzky played for Canada at the Winter Olympics in 1998.

In 2002, he ran the Canadian team that won the gold medal.

Nathan Chen
Figure skater Nathan Chen performs very difficult athletic routines. He's known as "the Quad King" for his mastery of quadruple jumps. He spins four times in the air in a single jump. In 2022, he won an Olympic gold medal.

Gerd Schönfelder
German skier Gerd Schönfelder is the most successful alpine skier at the Winter Paralympic Games. He lost his right arm and some left fingers in an accident in 1989. From 1992 through 2010, Schönfelder won 16 gold medals, four silvers, and two bronze at six Paralympics.

Terrific Tennis

Tennis is popular all around the world. It can be played by one person against a single opponent. It can also be played by teams of two players who compete as doubles partners.

Serena Williams

Serena Williams is one of the GOATs of tennis. She turned pro in 1995 and retired in 2022. Williams finished five different years ranked number one in women's tennis. She won 23 Grand Slam tournaments, more than any other woman in the modern era. Williams's fluid motion and body control gave her excellent power.

Roger Federer

Roger Federer began his pro tennis career in 1998. He played until 2022. At his best, Federer spent 237 straight weeks ranked number one in men's tennis. That's 77 more weeks than anyone else in history. Federer was the first men's tennis player to win 20 Grand Slam tournaments.

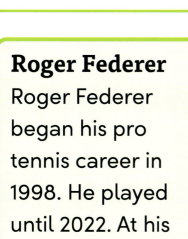

Grand Slam Tennis Tournaments
Australian Open (Melbourne)
French Open (Paris)
Wimbledon (London)
US Open (New York)

Solo Standouts

Few individual athletes are on their own more than a boxer facing an opponent in the ring. Golfers also compete on their own, but no one's trying to knock them out!

Muhammad Ali

Boxer Muhammad Ali had fast hands and was quick on his feet. In 1960, he won an Olympic gold medal. By 1964, he was heavyweight champion of the world. Ali became important as a civil rights activist. In 1967, he refused to fight in the Vietnam War. He was stripped of his heavyweight title and suspended from boxing until 1970. By 1974, Ali was champion again. He won the title for a third time in 1978.

Lydia Ko

Lydia Ko was born in Seoul, South Korea, but grew up in New Zealand. In 2012, she became the youngest winner ever on the Ladies Professional Golf Tour. Ko was only 15. Her 22 career wins to date are the most for any current LPGA player. Ko also won an Olympic gold medal in 2024.

Glossary

Activist
A person who works to bring about political or social change

Athlete
A person who is skilled at sports and other forms of exercise

Batting average
The total number of hits a baseball player gets, divided by the number of times they're up at bat

Century
In cricket, a score of 100 runs in a single game

Championship
A contest to determine an overall winner

Defense
The action of playing against another player or team and trying to stop them from scoring points

FIFA
Stands for the French name Fédération Internationale de Football Association and is the organization that governs soccer around the word

Grand Slam
Used to label the top four championships in a sport, especially tennis and golf

League
A group of sports teams that play against one another

Negro
An outdated word for Black people, which can be considered offensive today. It can be used when talking about history or referring to organizations such as the Negro Leagues.

Offense
The action of playing against another player or team and trying to score points

Pastime
An activity that people do regularly for enjoyment

Pro/professional
A person who gets paid to do something

Prosthesis
An artificial body part

Racism
Unfair treatment because of one's skin color or race

Test
In cricket, a format of the game that is played over five days

Tournament
A contest, or a series of contests, to determine a winner

Try
In rugby, moving the ball over the other team's goal line; worth five points

Index

Aaron, Hank 29
Acuña, Ronald, Jr. 29
Ali, Muhammad 44
Anderson, Patrick 37
Antetokounmpo, Giannis 36
baseball 28–31
basketball 34–37
Beckham, David 9
Betts, Mookie 29
Bikila, Abebe 25
Biles, Simone 24
Bjørgen, Marit 39
Bolt, Usain 22
Bonds, Barry 29
boxing 44
Brady, Tom 14, 15
Brown, Jim 17
Chen, Nathan 41
Clark, Caitlin 37
Cobb, Ty 31
cricket 32–33
cross-country skiing 39
cycling 21, 25
Farah, Mo 23
Federer, Roger 43
figure skating 41
football 14–17
Gibson, Josh 31
Gilgeous-Alexander, Shai 36
goalball 26
golf 45

Gretzky, Wayne 40
gymnastics 24
Hamm, Mia 11
Henderson, Gunnar 29
heptathlon 23
ice hockey 5, 40
ice skating 41
James, LeBron 34
Jokić, Nikola 36
Jordan, Michael 36
Judge, Aaron 29
Kenny, Jason 25
Kenny, Laura 25
Ko, Lydia 45
Ledecky, Katie 21
Lomu, Jonah 18
Mahomes, Patrick 16
marathon 25
Marta 13
Mays, Willie 31
Messi, Lionel 8, 9
Moore, Bobby 11
Negro Leagues 31
Ohtani, Shohei 28
Olympics
  Summer Olympics 6, 8, 11, 20–25, 44
  Winter Olympics 38–41
Paralympic Games 5, 21, 26–27, 37, 41
Peacock, Jonnie 27
Pelé 10, 11

Phelps, Michael 20
Red Roses 19
Rice, Jerry 17
Robinson, Jackie 30
Ronaldo, Cristiano 12, 13
Root, Joe 33
rugby 18–19
running 22–23, 25, 27
Ruth, Babe 29
Schönfelder, Gerd 41
Sinclair, Christine 13
skating 41
skiing 39, 41
snowboarding 38
soccer 8–13, 32
Storey, Sarah 21
swimming 20–21
Swoopes, Sheryl 35
Tendulkar, Sachin 32
tennis 42–43
Thiam, Nafissatou 23
track and field 22–23, 25, 27
Vieira da Silva, Marta 13
Virén, Lasse 23
Wembanyama, Victor 36
White, Shaun 38
Wilkinson, Jonny 19
Williams, Serena 42
Witt, Bobby, Jr. 29

47

Quiz

Answer the questions to see what you have learned. Check your answers in the key below.

1. Who is the only player to have played on three winning World Cup soccer teams?
2. How many times did Tom Brady win the Super Bowl?
3. Who won the most medals in Olympic history?
4. What sport has 2.5 billion fans around the world?
5. How old was Lydia Ko when she won her first LPGA tournament?

1. Pelé 2. Seven 3. Michael Phelps 4. Cricket 5. 15